I0007746

Mastering Salesforce Visualforce: A Guide to Developing Custom User Interfaces

Table of Contents:

Chapter 15: Advanced Lightning Web Components (LWC) Development

Chapter 1: Introduction to Visualforce

Welcome to the first chapter of "Mastering Salesforce Visualforce: A Comprehensive Guide to Developing Custom User Interfaces." In this chapter, we will introduce you to the world of Visualforce and help you understand its fundamental concepts. So, let's get started!

Section 1: What is Visualforce?

Visualforce is a powerful framework provided by Salesforce that allows developers to create custom user interfaces for their Salesforce applications. It enables you to build web pages, forms, and other user interface elements using a combination of HTML, CSS, and a unique syntax called Visualforce Markup Language (VFML).

Visualforce pages can interact with Salesforce data, leverage Apex (Salesforce's programming language), and provide a seamless user experience within the Salesforce ecosystem. It offers a high level of flexibility and customization, making it an indispensable tool for developers looking to enhance the user interface of their Salesforce applications.

Section 2: Benefits and Use Cases of Visualforce

Visualforce offers several benefits that make it a preferred choice for Salesforce developers. Here are some key advantages:

Customization: Visualforce allows you to create custom user interfaces tailored to your specific business requirements. You can design layouts, forms, and components that align with your organization's branding and user experience guidelines.

Data Integration: Visualforce seamlessly integrates with Salesforce's data model, enabling you to display, manipulate, and update data from Salesforce objects within your user interface. This tight integration streamlines user interactions and enhances productivity.

Extensibility: Visualforce provides extensive capabilities to extend the functionality of Salesforce. You can leverage Apex controllers and extensions to handle complex business logic, perform data manipulations, and interact with external systems.

Cross-Platform Compatibility: Visualforce pages are compatible with various web browsers and devices, ensuring a consistent user experience across different platforms.

Now, let's explore some common use cases where Visualforce can be utilized:

Creating custom data entry forms with business logic validations.

Building custom dashboards and reports to visualize Salesforce data.

Developing interactive pages for customer portals and partner communities.

Designing custom user interfaces for mobile applications using Salesforce Mobile SDK.

Section 3: Visualforce vs. Lightning Web Components

It's important to note that Salesforce has introduced a newer framework called Lightning Web Components (LWC) for building modern user interfaces. While Visualforce continues to be widely used, LWC offers enhanced performance, modularity, and a modern development experience.

In this book, our focus will primarily be on Visualforce, but we'll touch upon the integration of Visualforce with Lightning Experience and the migration to LWC.

Congratulations! You have completed the first chapter of "Mastering Salesforce Visualforce." In the next chapter, we will dive into the practical aspects of getting started with Visualforce, including setting up your Salesforce Developer Environment and creating your first Visualforce page.

Stay tuned and get ready to embark on an exciting journey into the world of Visualforce development!

Chapter 2: Getting Started with Visualforce

Welcome to Chapter 2 of "Mastering Salesforce Visualforce: A Comprehensive Guide to Developing Custom User Interfaces." In this chapter, we will guide you through the process of getting started with Visualforce. We'll cover everything from setting up your Salesforce Developer Environment to creating your first Visualforce page. Let's begin!

Section 1: Setting up Your Salesforce Developer Environment

Before you start developing with Visualforce, you'll need to set up your Salesforce Developer Environment. Follow these steps:

Sign up for a Salesforce Developer Account: Visit the Salesforce Developer website (developer.salesforce.com) and sign up for a free Developer Account. This account will provide you with a dedicated environment to develop and test your Visualforce applications.

Install a Code Editor: Choose a code editor that suits your preferences. Popular options include Visual Studio Code,

Sublime Text, and Atom. Install the editor of your choice and familiarize yourself with its features.

Install the Salesforce Extensions for Your Code Editor: Salesforce offers extensions for various code editors that provide helpful features like syntax highlighting, code completion, and Salesforce-specific tools. Install the appropriate Salesforce extension for your chosen code editor.

Set Up Salesforce CLI (Command-Line Interface): Salesforce CLI is a powerful tool that allows you to interact with your Salesforce environment from the command line. Install Salesforce CLI and authenticate it with your Salesforce Developer Account.

Section 2: Creating Your First Visualforce Page

Now that your development environment is set up, it's time to create your first Visualforce page. Follow these steps:

Launch your code editor and create a new file with a ".page" extension. For example, "MyFirstPage.page".

Begin with a Visualforce page template by typing "apex:page" and press Enter. This creates the basic structure of a Visualforce page.

Add a title to your page by inserting the "apex:sectionHeader" component and providing a value for the "title" attribute. For example:

<apex:sectionHeader title="My First Visualforce Page" />

Customize the content of your Visualforce page by adding components such as headers, forms, and tables. Utilize the Visualforce component tags to define the desired functionality and appearance.

Save the Visualforce page file and navigate to your Salesforce Developer Account.

In Salesforce, go to the "Setup" menu, and under "Develop," select "Pages."

Click on the "New" button to create a new Visualforce page.

Enter a suitable name and provide the content of your Visualforce page in the appropriate section.

Save the Visualforce page, and Salesforce will generate a URL that you can use to access your page.

Congratulations! You have created your first Visualforce page. Now, open the generated URL in a web browser to view your page in action.

Section 3: Understanding the Visualforce Syntax

Visualforce has its own syntax called Visualforce Markup Language (VFML), which combines HTML-like tags with Salesforce-specific attributes and expressions. Understanding the Visualforce syntax is crucial for effective development. Here are some key concepts to grasp:

Tags: Visualforce uses tags like "apex:page", "apex:form", and "apex:outputText" to define different components and elements on the page.

Attributes: Tags have attributes that control their behavior and appearance. For example, the "apex:page" tag has attributes like "showHeader" and "sidebar" to control the display of headers and sidebars.

Expressions: Visualforce allows you to embed expressions within tags to dynamically bind data or perform calculations. Expressions are enclosed within curly braces "{{ }}" and can reference variables, object fields, and formula expressions.

Controllers: Visualforce relies on controllers, either standard or custom, to handle the data and business logic associated with the page. Controllers are written in Apex, Salesforce's programming language.

Remember, practice makes perfect. Experiment with different Visualforce components and explore the Salesforce documentation for detailed information on available tags, attributes, and expressions.

Congratulations on completing Chapter 2! In the next chapter, we'll delve into Visualforce Controllers and learn how to connect the logic behind your Visualforce pages. Stay tuned!

Chapter 3: Visualforce Controllers

Welcome to Chapter 3 of "Mastering Salesforce Visualforce: A Comprehensive Guide to Developing Custom User Interfaces." In this chapter, we will dive into Visualforce controllers and learn how they are used to handle the data and business logic behind your Visualforce pages. Let's get started!

Section 1: Introduction to Visualforce Controllers

Visualforce controllers are an integral part of the Visualforce framework. They provide the logic and data manipulation capabilities required to interact with Salesforce data and deliver dynamic user experiences. There are two types of Visualforce controllers: standard controllers and custom controllers.

Standard Controllers: Salesforce provides standard controllers for most standard objects such as Accounts, Contacts, and Opportunities. These standard controllers automatically handle common operations like retrieving and saving data, making it easier to work with standard objects in Visualforce pages.

Custom Controllers: Custom controllers are Apex classes written by developers to define the behavior of Visualforce pages. They allow you to implement custom logic, perform complex calculations, and interact with external systems. Custom controllers provide greater flexibility and customization options for your Visualforce applications.

Section 2: Standard Controllers

Let's start by exploring standard controllers and how to use them in your Visualforce pages. Follow these steps:

Identify the Object: Determine the standard object you want to work with in your Visualforce page. For example, if you want to create a page for managing Contacts, you would use the Contact standard object.

Create the Visualforce Page: Create a new Visualforce page using the "apex:page" tag as discussed in Chapter 2.

Define the Standard Controller: Within the "apex:page" tag, specify the standard controller using the "standardController" attribute. For example:

```
<apex:page standardController="Contact">
```

Customize the Page: Add components and functionality to the Visualforce page using Visualforce tags and expressions. You can reference fields from the standard object using expressions like "{!Contact.FieldName}".

Save and Preview: Save the Visualforce page and preview it in your Salesforce Developer Account to see the page rendered with the data from the standard controller.

Section 3: Custom Controllers

Custom controllers provide a powerful way to implement complex business logic and handle custom functionality in your Visualforce pages. Let's explore how to create and use custom controllers:

Create the Custom Controller: In your Salesforce Developer Account, navigate to the Apex Classes section and create a new Apex class for your custom controller. Define the necessary methods and variables to handle the desired functionality.

Link the Custom Controller to the Visualforce Page: In the Visualforce page, specify the custom controller using the "controller" attribute within the "apex:page" tag. For example:

```
<apex:page controller="CustomController">
```

Access Data and Logic: Within the Visualforce page, you can now access the methods and variables defined in the custom controller using expressions like "{!methodname}" or "{!variableName}". This allows you to retrieve and manipulate data, perform calculations, and implement custom business logic.

Save and Preview: Save the Visualforce page and preview it in your Salesforce Developer Account to test the functionality implemented in the custom controller.

Section 4: Controller Extensions

Controller extensions provide a way to extend the functionality of standard controllers or other custom controllers. They allow you to add custom methods, variables, and logic to existing controllers without modifying the original controller code. Here's how you can create and use controller extensions:

Create the Controller Extension: Create a new Apex class that extends the standard or custom controller you want to extend. Add the desired methods and variables to the extension class.

Link the Controller Extension to the Visualforce Page: In the Visualforce page, specify the controller extension using the "extensions" attribute within the "apex:page" tag. For example:

```
<apex:page standardController="Contact"
extensions="ExtensionController">
```

Access Data and Logic: Within the Visualforce page, you can now access the methods and variables defined in the controller extension using expressions like "{!methodname}" or "{!variableName}". This allows you to extend the functionality of the underlying controller and implement custom behavior.

Save and Preview: Save the Visualforce page and preview it in your Salesforce Developer Account to test the extended functionality.

Section 5: Best Practices for Controllers

To ensure efficient and maintainable Visualforce development, consider the following best practices for working with controllers:

Keep controllers focused: Each controller should have a clear purpose and responsibility. Avoid creating monolithic controllers that handle too many functionalities.

Leverage controller extensions: Use controller extensions to extend the functionality of existing controllers, rather than duplicating code or modifying the original controller.

Use SOQL and DML effectively: When interacting with Salesforce data, use efficient SOQL queries and bulkified DML operations to minimize database access and optimize performance.

Implement unit tests: Write comprehensive unit tests for your controllers to ensure proper functionality and catch any issues early in the development cycle.

Congratulations on learning about Visualforce controllers! In the next chapter, we will explore Visualforce components and how to create reusable UI elements for your Visualforce pages. Stay tuned for an exciting journey into the world of Visualforce development!

Chapter 4: Visualforce Components

Welcome to Chapter 4 of "Mastering Salesforce Visualforce: A Comprehensive Guide to Developing Custom User Interfaces." In this chapter, we will explore Visualforce components and learn how to create reusable UI elements for your Visualforce pages. Visualforce components allow you to encapsulate functionality and design into modular building blocks. Let's dive in!

Section 1: Introduction to Visualforce Components

Visualforce components are reusable units of functionality and design that can be used across multiple Visualforce pages. They help you modularize your code, promote reusability, and maintain consistency in your user interface. Visualforce provides two types of components: standard components and custom components.

Standard Components: Salesforce provides a wide range of standard components, such as input fields, buttons, tables, and navigation elements. These components are ready to use and can be easily incorporated into your Visualforce pages.

Custom Components: Custom components are components created by developers to meet specific requirements. They allow you to build reusable elements tailored to your application's needs and design.

Section 2: Using Standard Components

Let's start by exploring the usage of standard components in your Visualforce pages:

Identify the Required Component: Determine the standard component you want to include in your Visualforce page. For example, if you need an input field to capture the user's name, you can use the <apex:inputText> component.

Include the Component: Add the component to your Visualforce page using the appropriate Visualforce tag. For example:

```
<apex:inputText value="{!contact.Name}" />
```

In this example, we're using the <apex:inputText> component to capture the user's name and bind it to the "Name" field of a Contact object.

Customize the Component: Utilize the available attributes of the standard component to customize its behavior and appearance. For example, you can specify attributes like "required", "label", and "maxlength" to control validation, labeling, and input length.

Save and Preview: Save the Visualforce page and preview it in your Salesforce Developer Account to see the standard component in action.

Section 3: Creating Custom Components

Custom components allow you to build reusable UI elements tailored to your specific needs. Here's how you can create and use custom components in your Visualforce pages:

Create the Custom Component: In your Salesforce Developer Account, navigate to the "Components" section and create a new Visualforce component. Define the required functionality and design within the component.

Utilize the Custom Component: In your Visualforce page, include the custom component using the

<c:ComponentName> syntax, where "ComponentName" is the name of your custom component.

Customize and Pass Parameters: Customize the appearance and behavior of the custom component by passing parameters to it. Parameters can be simple values, expressions, or references to other variables.

Save and Preview: Save the Visualforce page and preview it in your Salesforce Developer Account to test the functionality of your custom component.

Section 4: Reusing Components with Composition

Visualforce allows you to compose components and create more complex UI structures. Here's how you can reuse components by composition:

Identify the Components for Composition: Identify the components that you want to reuse and compose together to form a larger structure.

Define a Container Component: Create a new Visualforce component that serves as a container for the components to be composed. This container component will hold and organize the reusable components.

Include Reusable Components: Include the reusable components within the container component using the appropriate Visualforce tags. Pass any required parameters to the components.

Save and Utilize: Save the container component and utilize it in your Visualforce pages by including <c:ContainerComponent>.

Section 5: Best Practices for Using Components

Consider the following best practices when working with Visualforce components:

Encapsulate functionality: Design components that encapsulate specific functionality or features. This promotes reusability and modularity.

Utilize parameters: Leverage component parameters to make components more flexible and customizable.

Follow naming conventions: Name your components descriptively and consistently to ensure clarity and maintainability.

Test and validate: Test your components thoroughly to ensure they function as intended and handle different scenarios.

Congratulations on learning about Visualforce components! In the next chapter, we will delve into Visualforce navigation and explore different techniques to navigate between Visualforce pages. Get ready for more exciting discoveries in the world of Visualforce development!

Chapter 5: Visualforce Navigation

Welcome to Chapter 5 of "Mastering Salesforce Visualforce: A Comprehensive Guide to Developing Custom User Interfaces." In this chapter, we will explore Visualforce navigation techniques and learn how to navigate between different Visualforce pages. Navigation plays a crucial role in creating seamless user experiences within your Salesforce applications. Let's dive in!

Section 1: Understanding Visualforce Navigation

Visualforce provides various methods for navigating between different pages within your application. Understanding these navigation techniques will allow you to create intuitive and user-friendly interfaces. Let's explore the different approaches:

Link-Based Navigation: The most straightforward way to navigate between Visualforce pages is through hyperlinks or buttons that redirect users to a different page. This can be achieved using anchor tags <a href=""> or Visualforce <apex:commandLink> and <apex:commandButton> components.

Page Reference Navigation: Visualforce also provides a powerful mechanism called Page Reference that allows you to programmatically navigate to different pages. With Page References, you can dynamically set URL parameters, navigate to standard Salesforce pages, or even redirect to external URLs.

Navigation Events: Salesforce provides JavaScript-based navigation events that enable you to navigate programmatically without reloading the entire page. These events include sforce.one.navigateToURL(), sforce.one.navigateToSObject(), and sforce.one.createRecord(), among others.

Section 2: Link-Based Navigation

Let's start by exploring link-based navigation techniques using anchor tags and Visualforce components:

Anchor Tags: To create a hyperlink that navigates to a Visualforce page, use the HTML <a> tag and provide the URL of the target Visualforce page as the href attribute. For example:

<a href="/apex/TargetPage">Go to Target Page</a>

Ensure that the href attribute value begins with "/apex/" followed by the name or URL of the target Visualforce page.

Visualforce CommandLink and CommandButton: Instead of using plain HTML tags, Visualforce provides its own components for link-based navigation. Use

<apex:commandLink> and <apex:commandButton> components to create links and buttons that trigger navigation. For example:

<apex:commandLink action="/apex/TargetPage" value="Go to Target Page"/>

<apex:commandButton action="/apex/TargetPage" value="Go to Target Page"/>

Section 3: Page Reference Navigation

Page Reference provides a powerful way to navigate programmatically within your Visualforce application. Follow these steps to utilize Page References for navigation:

Create a Page Reference Object: In your custom controller or controller extension, create an instance of the Page Reference class. For example:

```
PageReference targetPage = new
PageReference('/apex/TargetPage');
```

Set Parameters (Optional): If your target page requires URL parameters, use the getParameters() method of the Page Reference object to set the desired parameters. For example:

```
targetPage.getParameters().put('paramName',
'paramValue');
```

Redirect to the Target Page: To navigate to the target Visualforce page, use the setRedirect() and return statements in your controller method. For example:

```
targetPage.setRedirect(true);

return targetPage;
```

Section 4: Navigation Events

Salesforce provides JavaScript-based navigation events that enable seamless navigation within your Visualforce pages. Here's an overview of some commonly used navigation events:

sforce.one.navigateToURL(): This event allows you to navigate to a specified URL within Salesforce or even to external websites.

sforce.one.navigateToSObject(): Use this event to navigate to a specific record detail page within Salesforce.

sforce.one.createRecord(): This event enables you to open a new record creation page for a specified Salesforce object.

Utilize these navigation events by calling them within JavaScript functions triggered by user interactions or other events.

Section 5: Best Practices for Visualforce Navigation

Consider the following best practices when implementing Visualforce navigation:

Keep navigation intuitive: Ensure that the navigation flow in your application is logical and intuitive for users to follow.

Validate user input: When navigating based on user input, validate and sanitize the input to avoid any security risks or unexpected behavior.

Leverage Page References: Use Page References for programmatic navigation, as they provide flexibility and control over the navigation flow.

Optimize performance: Consider the performance impact of navigation events and choose the appropriate approach based on the specific requirements of your application.

Congratulations! You've learned various techniques for navigating between Visualforce pages. In the next chapter, we will explore Visualforce data binding and learn how to display and manipulate data in your custom user interfaces.

Get ready for an exciting journey into Visualforce data management!

Chapter 6: Visualforce Data Binding

Welcome to Chapter 6 of "Mastering Salesforce Visualforce: A Comprehensive Guide to Developing Custom User Interfaces." In this chapter, we will explore Visualforce data binding and learn how to display and manipulate data within your custom user interfaces. Data binding allows you to seamlessly integrate Salesforce data into your Visualforce pages. Let's dive in!

Section 1: Introduction to Data Binding

Data binding is a fundamental concept in Visualforce that enables you to connect your user interface components with Salesforce data. By binding your components to data, you can display, manipulate, and update the data seamlessly. Visualforce offers several ways to achieve data binding, including standard data binding, expressions, and binding to Apex controllers.

Section 2: Standard Data Binding

Let's start by exploring the standard data binding mechanism in Visualforce. With standard data binding, you can directly bind components to fields of a Salesforce object. Follow these steps to utilize standard data binding:

Identify the Salesforce Object: Determine the Salesforce object from which you want to display data. For example, if you want to display contact details, the Salesforce object would be the Contact object.

Bind Components to Fields: Use the appropriate Visualforce component and bind it to the desired field using the value attribute. For example, to display the contact's name, use the <apex:outputText> component as follows:

```
<apex:outputText value="{!contact.Name}" />
```

In this example, contact represents an instance of the Contact object, and Name is the field you want to bind to.

Display and Manipulate Data: Save the Visualforce page and preview it in your Salesforce Developer Account. The component will display the value of the bound field from the specified Salesforce object.

Section 3: Expressions

Visualforce allows you to use expressions to dynamically display and manipulate data within your components. Expressions are enclosed within curly braces ({!}) and can reference variables, fields, and formulas. Let's explore how to use expressions for data binding:

Define Variables: In your controller or controller extension, define variables that store the data you want to display or manipulate. For example, you can define a variable myVariable as follows:

```
public String myVariable { get; set; }
```

Bind Components to Variables: Use expressions to bind components to the defined variables. For example, to display the value of myVariable, use the <apex:outputText> component as follows:

```
<apex:outputText value="{!myVariable}" />
```

Set Values in the Controller: In your controller or controller extension, set the values of the variables as needed. The bound components will dynamically display the updated values.

Section 4: Binding to Apex Controllers

Visualforce allows you to bind components directly to methods and variables in your Apex controllers or controller extensions. This provides a powerful way to handle data manipulation and logic within your Visualforce pages. Follow these steps to bind components to Apex controllers:

Create Controller Methods: In your Apex controller or controller extension, define methods that handle data manipulation or logic. For example, you can create a method getData() that returns the data you want to display.

Bind Components to Controller Methods: Use expressions to bind components to the controller methods. For example, to display the data returned by getData(), use the <apex:outputText> component as follows:

```
<apex:outputText value="{!getData()}" />
```

Save and Preview: Save the Visualforce page and preview it in your Salesforce Developer Account. The component will display the data returned by the bound controller method.

Section 5: Data Manipulation and Update

Visualforce provides various components and techniques for data manipulation and update. Some commonly used components include <apex:inputText>, <apex:selectList>, and <apex:commandButton>. By binding these components to fields or variables, you can capture user input and update the data accordingly.

Utilize appropriate controller methods or actions in conjunction with these components to handle data updates and perform any required business logic.

Section 6: Best Practices for Data Binding

Consider the following best practices when working with data binding in Visualforce:

Keep data binding simple: Avoid complex expressions and keep data binding straightforward for readability and maintainability.

Follow naming conventions: Use descriptive names for variables, fields, and methods to ensure clarity and ease of understanding.

Validate user input: Implement validation logic to ensure the accuracy and integrity of data entered by users.

Utilize bulkified operations: When performing data updates, use bulkified operations to handle multiple records efficiently and avoid governor limits.

Congratulations! You have learned about Visualforce data binding and how to display and manipulate data within your custom user interfaces. In the next chapter, we will explore Visualforce styling and formatting, allowing you to enhance the visual appeal of your pages. Get ready to create visually stunning user interfaces with Visualforce!

Chapter 7: Visualforce Styling and Formatting

Welcome to Chapter 7 of "Mastering Salesforce Visualforce: A Comprehensive Guide to Developing Custom User Interfaces." In this chapter, we will explore Visualforce styling and formatting techniques to enhance the visual appeal of your pages. Visualforce provides several options for customizing the look and feel of your user interfaces. Let's dive in!

Section 1: CSS Styling in Visualforce

Cascading Style Sheets (CSS) is a powerful tool for styling HTML elements, and Visualforce allows you to leverage CSS to style your user interfaces. Follow these steps to apply CSS styling to your Visualforce pages:

Create a CSS File: Create a new CSS file in your preferred code editor and save it with a ".css" extension. For example, "styles.css".

Define CSS Styles: Within the CSS file, define the styles for the HTML elements or Visualforce components you want to customize. Use CSS selectors to target specific elements or classes. For example:

```css
.myClass {

  color: blue;

  font-size: 16px;

}
```

Link the CSS File: In your Visualforce page, link the CSS file by adding a <link> tag within the <head> section. For example:

```html
<head>

  <link rel="stylesheet" type="text/css"
href="{!URLFOR($Resource.StaticResources, 'styles.css')}"/>

</head>
```

Ensure that the href attribute value points to the correct location of your CSS file. In this example, we assume the CSS file is stored as a static resource named "StaticResources".

Apply CSS Classes: Apply CSS classes to the desired HTML elements or Visualforce components by adding the styleClass attribute and providing the class name.

For example:

```
<apex:outputText value="Hello World!"
styleClass="myClass"/>
```

Section 2: Customizing Page Layouts

Visualforce allows you to customize the layout of your pages to create visually appealing user interfaces. You can utilize HTML elements, CSS, and Visualforce components to achieve the desired layout. Consider the following techniques:

HTML Structure: Use HTML elements like <div>, <span>, and <table> to structure your page layout. Apply CSS styles and classes to these elements to control their positioning, spacing, and alignment.

CSS Grids: Leverage CSS grid systems or frameworks like Bootstrap or Salesforce Lightning Design System (SLDS) to create responsive and consistent page layouts. These grid systems provide pre-defined CSS classes and styles for easy grid-based layout design.

Visualforce Components: Utilize Visualforce components like <apex:pageBlock>, <apex:pageBlockSection>, and

<apex:outputPanel> to create structured and organized sections within your page layout.

Section 3: Using Salesforce Design System (SLDS)

Salesforce Lightning Design System (SLDS) provides a set of CSS styles, icons, and components that adhere to the Salesforce user experience guidelines. Utilizing SLDS in your Visualforce pages ensures consistency with the Salesforce Lightning Experience. Follow these steps to use SLDS in your Visualforce pages:

Include SLDS Resources: Add the necessary SLDS resources to your Visualforce page by including the required CSS files and JavaScript files. You can either host the files locally or reference them directly from Salesforce's CDN. For example:

```
<link rel="stylesheet"
href="https://www.lightningdesignsystem.com/assets/styles
/salesforce-lightning-design-system.min.css"/>

<script
src="https://www.lightningdesignsystem.com/assets/scripts/
salesforce-lightning-design-system.min.js"></script>
```

Apply SLDS Styles: Apply SLDS styles and classes to your HTML elements or Visualforce components to align with the Salesforce user experience. Refer to the SLDS documentation for a comprehensive list of available styles, components, and usage guidelines.

Section 4: Best Practices for Visualforce Styling

Consider the following best practices when styling your Visualforce pages:

Maintain consistency: Follow a consistent styling approach across your application to create a unified user experience.

Optimize for responsiveness: Design your pages to be responsive and accessible across different devices and screen sizes.

Minimize inline styles: Prefer external CSS files over inline styles to promote maintainability and reusability.

Leverage SLDS: Utilize Salesforce Lightning Design System (SLDS) to align with Salesforce's design guidelines and ensure a consistent look and feel.

Congratulations! You have learned about Visualforce styling and formatting techniques. In the next chapter, we will explore Visualforce validation and error handling, enabling you to validate user input and handle errors effectively. Get ready to enhance the functionality and reliability of your Visualforce applications!

Chapter 8: Visualforce Validation and Error Handling

Welcome to Chapter 8 of "Mastering Salesforce Visualforce: A Comprehensive Guide to Developing Custom User Interfaces." In this chapter, we will explore Visualforce validation and error handling techniques to ensure data integrity and provide meaningful error messages to users. Validation and error handling are essential aspects of building robust and user-friendly applications. Let's dive in!

Section 1: Implementing Validation Rules

Validation rules allow you to define criteria for data input and ensure that the entered values meet specific requirements. Visualforce provides various ways to implement validation rules. Follow these steps to implement validation rules in your Visualforce pages:

Determine the Validation Criteria: Identify the validation criteria for the data input. For example, you might want to ensure that a text field is not left blank or that a numeric value falls within a certain range.

Server-Side Validation with Apex: Implement server-side validation logic in your Apex controller or controller extension. In the controller method responsible for processing the data, write the necessary validation rules using conditional statements and Apex logic.

Displaying Validation Errors: If a validation rule is not met, use the ApexPages.addMessage() method to add an error message to the Visualforce page. For example:

```
if (validationRuleNotMet) {

    ApexPages.addMessage(new
ApexPages.Message(ApexPages.Severity.ERROR, 'Validation
Rule Not Met!'));

}
```

Displaying Error Messages on the Page: Add a Visualforce component like <apex:pageMessages> to display the error messages on the Visualforce page. For example:

```
<apex:pageMessages />
```

Place this component wherever you want the error messages to appear on the page.

Section 2: Handling Exceptions in Visualforce

Exception handling is crucial to handle unexpected errors and exceptions that may occur during the execution of your Visualforce pages. Follow these steps to implement exception handling:

Identify Potential Exception Points: Identify the parts of your Visualforce page or controller where exceptions may occur. This can include data retrieval, DML operations, external system integrations, or custom logic.

Use Try-Catch Blocks: Surround the code that may throw an exception with a try-catch block. In the catch block, handle the exception appropriately. For example:

```
try {
    // Code that may throw an exception
} catch (Exception e) {
    // Exception handling logic
    ApexPages.addMessage(new
ApexPages.Message(ApexPages.Severity.ERROR, 'An error
occurred: ' + e.getMessage()));
}
```

Displaying Error Messages: Similar to validation errors, use <apex:pageMessages> to display the error messages on the Visualforce page.

Section 3: Visualforce Remote Objects for Client-Side Validation

Visualforce Remote Objects allow you to perform client-side validation using JavaScript. With Remote Objects, you can validate user input before submitting it to the server. Follow these steps to implement client-side validation using Remote Objects:

Include the Remote Objects JavaScript Library: Add the Remote Objects JavaScript library to your Visualforce page. For example:

```
<script src="/soap/ajax/39.0/connection.js"
type="text/javascript"></script>

<script src="/soap/ajax/39.0/remote.js"
type="text/javascript"></script>
```

Define Remote Objects: Define the Remote Objects in JavaScript using the sforce.connection.remoteObjectModel namespace. This allows you to interact with Salesforce objects and perform validation on the client-side.

Implement Validation Logic: Use JavaScript to validate the user input based on your defined criteria. Display appropriate error messages or prevent form submission if the validation fails.

Server-Side Validation (Optional): Although client-side validation can improve user experience, it is crucial to implement server-side validation as well to ensure data integrity and security. Perform server-side validation in your Apex controller or controller extension as discussed in Section 1.

Section 4: Best Practices for Validation and Error Handling

Consider the following best practices for implementing validation and error handling in your Visualforce pages:

Validate input on both client-side and server-side to ensure data integrity and security.

Provide clear and user-friendly error messages that help users understand and correct the issues.

Leverage Visualforce components like <apex:pageMessages> to display error messages consistently.

Follow exception handling best practices, such as logging error details for debugging purposes and providing relevant error messages to users.

Test different scenarios, including valid and invalid inputs, to ensure your validation and error handling mechanisms work as expected.

Congratulations! You have learned how to implement validation rules, handle exceptions, and provide meaningful error messages in your Visualforce applications. In the next chapter, we will explore Visualforce testing and debugging techniques, enabling you to ensure the quality and reliability of your Visualforce code. Get ready to become a proficient Visualforce developer!

Chapter 9: Visualforce Testing and Debugging

Welcome to Chapter 9 of "Mastering Salesforce Visualforce: A Comprehensive Guide to Developing Custom User Interfaces." In this chapter, we will explore Visualforce testing and debugging techniques to ensure the quality and reliability of your Visualforce code. Testing and debugging are crucial steps in the development process to identify and fix issues before deploying your applications. Let's dive in!

Section 1: Unit Testing in Visualforce

Unit testing is a critical aspect of ensuring the correctness and functionality of your Visualforce code. Apex provides a robust testing framework that allows you to write automated tests for your Visualforce controllers and controller extensions. Follow these steps to perform unit testing in Visualforce:

Create a Test Class: In your Salesforce Developer Account, create an Apex test class that is dedicated to testing your Visualforce code. The test class should have methods that cover different scenarios and test the desired functionality.

Write Test Methods: Write test methods within the test class to cover different aspects of your Visualforce code. Test methods should simulate user interactions, set up test data, and verify expected outcomes using assertions.

Test Data Setup: In each test method, create the necessary test data to replicate real-world scenarios. This may involve creating mock records, populating fields, and ensuring the data represents the conditions you want to test.

Invoke the Visualforce Code: Within your test methods, invoke the Visualforce code by instantiating the controller or controller extension and calling the relevant methods or actions. Pass any required parameters as needed.

Assertions and Verification: After invoking the Visualforce code, use assertions to verify the expected outcomes. Assertions allow you to compare actual results with expected results and determine if the code is functioning correctly.

Run the Tests: Execute the unit tests in Salesforce by running the test class. This will validate the functionality of your Visualforce code and provide feedback on any errors or failures.

Section 2: Debugging Techniques

Debugging is an essential skill for identifying and resolving issues in your Visualforce code. Visualforce provides various debugging techniques to help you troubleshoot problems effectively. Follow these techniques for effective Visualforce debugging:

System.debug Statements: Utilize System.debug() statements in your Apex controllers or controller extensions to output debug information to the Developer Console. This allows you to inspect variable values, execution paths, and other relevant information during runtime.

Debugging Visualforce Pages: Enable debugging for Visualforce pages by adding the debug="true" attribute to the <apex:page> tag. This displays detailed debug information at the bottom of the Visualforce page when accessed.

Developer Console: Use the Developer Console, a powerful debugging tool provided by Salesforce, to monitor and debug your Visualforce code. It allows you to view debug logs, execute anonymous Apex code, and analyze performance.

Debug Logs: Enable debug logging for your Visualforce pages to capture detailed logs of the runtime execution. Use the Debug Logs section in Salesforce to view and analyze these logs, helping you identify errors and understand code behavior.

Section 3: Best Practices for Testing and Debugging

Consider the following best practices for testing and debugging your Visualforce code:

Write comprehensive unit tests to cover different scenarios and edge cases.

Use meaningful test data to replicate real-world scenarios and validate the functionality of your Visualforce code.

Leverage assertions to validate expected outcomes and ensure the correctness of your code.

Regularly review debug logs and debug output to identify potential issues and troubleshoot errors.

Use the Developer Console and other debugging tools provided by Salesforce to streamline your debugging process.

Continuously improve your testing and debugging skills by exploring new techniques and staying updated with best practices.

Congratulations! You have learned about Visualforce testing and debugging techniques. In the next chapter, we will explore Visualforce security and best practices to protect your applications and sensitive data. Get ready to enhance the security of your Visualforce applications!

Chapter 10: Visualforce Security Best Practices

Welcome to Chapter 10 of "Mastering Salesforce Visualforce: A Comprehensive Guide to Developing Custom User Interfaces." In this chapter, we will explore Visualforce security and best practices to protect your applications and sensitive data. Security is a critical aspect of any application development, and understanding Visualforce security best practices is essential for building secure applications. Let's dive in!

Section 1: Cross-Site Scripting (XSS) Prevention

Cross-Site Scripting (XSS) is a common web application vulnerability that allows attackers to inject malicious scripts into web pages viewed by users. Visualforce provides built-in measures to prevent XSS attacks. Follow these best practices to prevent XSS vulnerabilities in your Visualforce applications:

Utilize Visualforce Markup: Visualforce automatically escapes user input by default, preventing the execution of malicious scripts. Always use Visualforce markup to display user-generated or dynamic content on your pages.

Avoid Unsafe HTML Tags: If you need to include HTML tags in your Visualforce pages, ensure that you only use trusted and safe tags. Avoid allowing user input that includes potentially dangerous HTML tags.

Sanitize User Input: Validate and sanitize user input on the server-side to remove any potentially harmful characters or scripts. Utilize Apex methods like String.escapeHtml4() or custom sanitization techniques to ensure that user input is safe to display.

Section 2: Object and Field Level Security

Visualforce integrates with Salesforce's robust security model, which includes object and field level security. Follow these best practices to ensure proper object and field level security in your Visualforce applications:

Respect Field Level Security: Always respect field level security settings when displaying or manipulating data in your Visualforce pages. Verify that the current user has the appropriate permissions to view or edit specific fields.

Leverage Field Accessibility: Utilize field accessibility properties like isAccessible() and isUpdateable() in your Apex controllers or controller extensions to check if a user has the necessary access rights before performing any operations.

Use Schema Describes: Utilize Schema Describes to dynamically determine the object and field accessibility and adjust your Visualforce page behavior accordingly. Schema Describes provide valuable information about the metadata of your Salesforce objects.

Section 3: Preventing Data Access Violations

Ensuring that users can only access the data they are authorized to view is crucial for maintaining data privacy and security. Follow these best practices to prevent data access violations in your Visualforce applications:

Implement Record-Level Access Control: Use Apex code in your controller or controller extension to enforce record-level access control. Leverage sharing rules, record types, or custom logic to restrict access to records based on user profiles or roles.

Avoid Hardcoding IDs: Avoid hardcoding record IDs in your Visualforce pages, as it can potentially expose sensitive data.

Instead, use dynamic queries or Apex code to retrieve records based on user context or criteria.

Utilize Apex Sharing: Leverage Apex sharing to programmatically share or revoke access to records based on your business requirements. Use sharing rules or manual sharing methods to control data visibility.

Section 4: Protecting Sensitive Data

Visualforce provides mechanisms to protect sensitive data and prevent unauthorized access. Follow these best practices to protect sensitive data in your Visualforce applications:

Use Secure Apex APIs: Utilize secure Apex APIs provided by Salesforce, such as Crypto class for encryption and Auth class for authentication, to protect sensitive data in your Visualforce applications.

Implement Field-Level Encryption: Leverage platform encryption or custom encryption techniques to encrypt sensitive data fields in your Salesforce objects. Ensure that the encrypted data is appropriately handled in your Visualforce pages.

Secure Data Transmission: Use secure protocols like HTTPS to encrypt data transmitted between the client and the server. Enable Secure Socket Layer (SSL) or Transport Layer Security (TLS) to ensure secure communication.

Section 5: Best Practices for Visualforce Security

Consider the following best practices to enhance the security of your Visualforce applications:

Regularly review and apply Salesforce security updates and patches to protect against new vulnerabilities and exploits.

Enforce strong password policies and encourage users to use unique and complex passwords.

Implement two-factor authentication (2FA) to add an extra layer of security to user logins.

Educate developers and users about common security threats and best practices to promote a security-conscious culture.

Continuously monitor and review access controls, permissions, and security configurations to detect and address potential vulnerabilities.

Congratulations! You have learned about Visualforce security best practices. In the next chapter, we will explore advanced Visualforce techniques, including custom controllers, extensions, and more. Get ready to level up your Visualforce development skills!

Chapter 11: Advanced Visualforce Techniques

Welcome to Chapter 11 of "Mastering Salesforce Visualforce: A Comprehensive Guide to Developing Custom User Interfaces." In this chapter, we will explore advanced Visualforce techniques to take your development skills to the next level. We will cover topics such as custom controllers, controller extensions, asynchronous operations, and more. Let's dive in!

Section 1: Custom Controllers and Controller Extensions

Custom controllers and controller extensions provide powerful ways to extend the functionality of your Visualforce pages and handle complex business logic. Let's explore how to create and utilize custom controllers and controller extensions:

Custom Controllers: A custom controller is an Apex class that provides data and logic to a Visualforce page. To create a custom controller, define an Apex class with methods and properties that handle data manipulation, calculations, and interactions with Salesforce objects. Associate the custom controller with your Visualforce page using the controller attribute. For example:

```
<apex:page controller="CustomController">
```

Controller Extensions: A controller extension allows you to enhance an existing standard or custom controller's functionality. To create a controller extension, define an Apex class that extends the base controller's functionality by adding additional methods, properties, or overrides. Associate the controller extension with your Visualforce page using the extensions attribute. For example:

```
<apex:page standardController="Account"
extensions="ExtensionController">
```

Section 2: Asynchronous Operations with Visualforce

Asynchronous operations are essential for performing time-consuming tasks without blocking the user interface. Visualforce provides mechanisms to execute code asynchronously using JavaScript remoting and Apex Batch Apex. Let's explore these techniques:

JavaScript Remoting: JavaScript remoting allows you to make asynchronous server calls from your Visualforce page using JavaScript. By utilizing the @RemoteAction annotation in your Apex class, you can expose methods that can be invoked asynchronously from JavaScript. This enables you to perform server-side operations without refreshing the entire page.

Apex Batch Apex: Batch Apex allows you to process large volumes of data in smaller chunks asynchronously. By implementing the Database.Batchable interface in your Apex class, you can define the logic to process records in batches. This is particularly useful when working with large data sets that cannot be processed in a single transaction.

Section 3: Visualforce Component Reference

Visualforce provides a vast library of pre-built components that you can leverage to enhance your user interfaces. Here are some commonly used components:

<apex:pageBlock>: Displays a section of content with a title.

<apex:pageBlockTable>: Renders a table to display data in rows and columns.

<apex:form>: Wraps a set of form controls to enable data submission and validation.

<apex:actionFunction>: Invokes an Apex method from JavaScript without a page refresh.

<apex:selectList>: Creates a dropdown list for selecting an item from a list of options.

<apex:outputPanel>: Groups components together for conditional rendering or JavaScript manipulation.

Section 4: Visualforce Performance Optimization

Optimizing Visualforce performance is crucial for delivering responsive and efficient user interfaces. Consider the following best practices for performance optimization:

Minimize the use of server-side view state by using the transient keyword and storing data in Apex classes instead.

Utilize pagination and lazy loading techniques to load data incrementally and improve page load times.

Leverage Visualforce caching mechanisms like <apex:cache> to cache frequently accessed data or components.

Optimize queries by using selective and efficient SOQL queries, leveraging indexes, and bulkifying operations.

Compress and minify CSS and JavaScript files to reduce file sizes and improve page load times.

Section 5: Best Practices for Advanced Visualforce Development

Consider the following best practices when working with advanced Visualforce techniques:

Follow separation of concerns by separating business logic from presentation logic in your controllers and extensions.

Utilize design patterns like MVC (Model-View-Controller) to structure your Visualforce code for better organization and maintainability.

Implement error handling and exception management to gracefully handle unexpected issues and provide meaningful feedback to users.

Continuously test and optimize your Visualforce code to ensure performance, scalability, and maintainability.

Congratulations! You have learned advanced Visualforce techniques, including custom controllers, controller extensions, asynchronous operations, and performance optimization. In the next chapter, we will explore integration options with Visualforce, allowing you to integrate external systems and services into your Salesforce applications. Get ready to unlock new possibilities with Visualforce integration!

Chapter 12: Visualforce Integration

Welcome to Chapter 12 of "Mastering Salesforce Visualforce: A Comprehensive Guide to Developing Custom User Interfaces." In this chapter, we will explore Visualforce integration options, which allow you to integrate external systems and services into your Salesforce applications. Integrating with external systems enables you to extend the capabilities of your Visualforce pages and create seamless user experiences. Let's dive in!

Section 1: Outbound Integration with Web Services

Visualforce allows you to integrate with external web services using various protocols such as SOAP, REST, and HTTP. Follow these steps to perform outbound integration:

Identify the Web Service: Determine the external web service you want to integrate with. This can be a SOAP-based web service, a RESTful API, or any other web service that exposes endpoints for data exchange.

Generate the Web Service Client: If the external web service is SOAP-based, you can use the Salesforce WSDL2Apex tool to generate Apex classes that represent the web service's data structures and operations. For RESTful APIs, you can use Apex's HttpRequest and HttpResponse classes to send HTTP requests and parse the response.

Invoke the Web Service: Utilize the generated Apex classes or custom Apex logic to invoke the web service's operations. This may involve sending SOAP requests, making RESTful API calls, or interacting with the web service's endpoints as per its documentation.

Process the Response: Handle the response received from the web service by parsing and extracting the relevant data. You can then utilize this data within your Visualforce pages to display or further process the integrated information.

Section 2: Inbound Integration with Apex Web Services

Inbound integration allows external systems to communicate with your Visualforce pages by invoking Apex web services. This enables you to expose custom functionality and data to external systems. Follow these steps to perform inbound integration:

Define the Apex Web Service: Create an Apex class that defines the methods and logic you want to expose as a web service. Use the webservice keyword to define methods that can be invoked by external systems. For example:

```
global class MyWebService {

    webservice static String processData(String input) {

        // Process the input and return a response

    }

}
```

Generate the WSDL or REST Endpoint: For SOAP-based web services, Salesforce automatically generates the WSDL (Web Services Description Language) file that describes your Apex web service. For RESTful web services, you can define custom endpoints using Apex's @RestResource annotation.

Provide the WSDL or Endpoint to External Systems: Share the generated WSDL file or REST endpoint with the external systems that will be consuming your Apex web service. They can then utilize the provided details to invoke your web service and exchange data.

Process Incoming Requests: In your Apex web service class, implement the necessary logic to process incoming requests and perform any required actions based on the data received. You can leverage Salesforce's built-in capabilities, access Salesforce objects, or interact with external systems to fulfill the requests.

Section 3: Integration with JavaScript Libraries

Visualforce allows you to integrate with various JavaScript libraries and frameworks to enhance your user interfaces and functionality. Follow these steps to integrate JavaScript libraries into your Visualforce pages:

Include the Library: Add the necessary JavaScript library by including the library's script file in your Visualforce page. You can host the file locally or reference it from a content delivery network (CDN). For example:

```
<script src="https://example.com/library.js"></script>
```

Leverage JavaScript Remoting: Utilize JavaScript remoting to communicate between your Visualforce pages and the JavaScript library. JavaScript remoting allows you to make asynchronous server calls from JavaScript and retrieve data or invoke Apex methods.

Integrate with Visualforce Components: Integrate the JavaScript library with Visualforce components by leveraging JavaScript functions, event listeners, and DOM manipulation. You can bind JavaScript actions to Visualforce components, handle user interactions, and update the UI dynamically.

Section 4: Best Practices for Visualforce Integration

Consider the following best practices for integrating external systems and services with Visualforce:

Use secure protocols like HTTPS for communication with external systems to protect sensitive data.

Implement proper error handling and exception management to gracefully handle integration failures and display meaningful error messages.

Validate and sanitize data exchanged between Visualforce and external systems to prevent security vulnerabilities.

Leverage Apex's governor limits awareness to ensure that your integration operations stay within the allowed limits.

Continuously monitor and test your integrations to ensure their functionality and performance.

Congratulations! You have learned about Visualforce integration options, including outbound integration with web services, inbound integration with Apex web services, and integration with JavaScript libraries. In the next chapter, we will explore mobile optimization techniques for Visualforce, enabling you to deliver exceptional user experiences on mobile devices. Get ready to make your Visualforce applications mobile-friendly!

Chapter 13: Mobile Optimization with Visualforce

Welcome to Chapter 13 of "Mastering Salesforce Visualforce: A Comprehensive Guide to Developing Custom User Interfaces." In this chapter, we will explore mobile optimization techniques for Visualforce, allowing you to deliver exceptional user experiences on mobile devices. As mobile usage continues to rise, it is crucial to optimize your Visualforce applications for mobile platforms. Let's dive in!

Section 1: Responsive Design Principles

Responsive design is an approach that enables your Visualforce pages to adapt and display properly across different screen sizes and devices. Follow these principles to achieve responsive design:

Fluid Grid Layout: Use a fluid grid layout system that allows your page elements to resize proportionally based on the screen width. Leverage CSS frameworks like Bootstrap or Salesforce Lightning Design System (SLDS) to implement responsive grid systems.

Flexible Images: Ensure that images in your Visualforce pages are flexible and can resize or scale based on the device's screen size. Utilize CSS techniques like max-width: 100% to make images responsive.

Media Queries: Implement media queries in your CSS to define different styles based on the screen width or device type. This allows you to customize the layout, font sizes, and other visual aspects for specific screen sizes.

Section 2: Touch-Friendly Interactions

Optimizing your Visualforce pages for touch interactions enhances the user experience on mobile devices. Consider the following touch-friendly techniques:

Increase Tap Targets: Make buttons, links, and interactive elements larger to ensure they are easy to tap with a finger. The recommended minimum target size is around 48x48 pixels.

Eliminate Hover Dependencies: Mobile devices do not support hover interactions like desktops. Ensure that your Visualforce pages do not rely heavily on hover-based functionality to avoid usability issues on touch devices.

Use Touch Gestures: Leverage touch gestures like swiping, pinching, and tapping to provide intuitive and interactive experiences. JavaScript libraries like Hammer.js can assist in implementing touch gestures.

Section 3: Performance Optimization for Mobile

Optimizing the performance of your Visualforce pages is crucial for delivering a smooth and fast experience on mobile devices. Follow these best practices for mobile performance optimization:

Minify and Compress: Minify your CSS and JavaScript files to reduce their file sizes. Compress images to minimize their impact on page load times. Utilize tools like CSS minifiers, JavaScript compressors, and image optimization plugins to achieve this.

Reduce HTTP Requests: Minimize the number of HTTP requests by combining CSS and JavaScript files, leveraging browser caching, and utilizing CSS sprites for icons or images.

Lazy Loading: Implement lazy loading techniques to load images, data, or content on-demand as users scroll. This prevents unnecessary loading of resources that are not immediately visible to the user.

Section 4: Testing and Emulating Mobile Devices

Testing your Visualforce pages on actual mobile devices is essential to ensure a seamless mobile experience. Consider the following approaches for testing and emulating mobile devices:

Device Testing: Test your Visualforce pages on a variety of actual mobile devices with different screen sizes, operating systems, and browsers. This allows you to identify any specific issues or inconsistencies on different devices.

Browser Developer Tools: Leverage browser developer tools like Google Chrome's DevTools or Safari's Web Inspector to emulate mobile devices. These tools provide device emulation modes that simulate various mobile platforms and screen sizes.

Responsive Design Testing Tools: Utilize responsive design testing tools such as BrowserStack or Responsive Design Checker to preview and test your Visualforce pages on multiple devices simultaneously.

Section 5: Best Practices for Mobile Optimization

Consider the following best practices for mobile optimization with Visualforce:

Prioritize mobile-first design to ensure that your Visualforce pages are optimized for mobile devices from the start.

Use a modular and component-based approach in your Visualforce code to promote reusability and adaptability across different screen sizes.

Continuously test and iterate your mobile optimizations to ensure compatibility with the latest mobile devices and browsers.

Gather user feedback and monitor analytics to identify areas for improvement and make data-driven decisions in your mobile optimization efforts.

Congratulations! You have learned mobile optimization techniques for Visualforce. In the next chapter, we will explore Lightning Web Components (LWC) and how you can leverage them to build modern, interactive user interfaces. Get ready to embrace the power of LWC in your Visualforce development journey!

Chapter 14: Introduction to Lightning Web Components (LWC)

Welcome to Chapter 14 of "Mastering Salesforce Visualforce: A Comprehensive Guide to Developing Custom User Interfaces." In this chapter, we will introduce Lightning Web Components (LWC) and explore how you can leverage them to build modern, interactive user interfaces. LWC is a cutting-edge technology that provides a powerful framework for building components in Salesforce. Let's dive in!

Section 1: Understanding Lightning Web Components (LWC)

Lightning Web Components (LWC) is a programming model and framework for building web components in Salesforce. LWC utilizes modern web standards like JavaScript, HTML, and CSS to deliver performant and reusable components. Here are some key aspects of LWC:

Component-Based Architecture: LWC follows a component-based architecture, allowing you to build complex user interfaces by combining smaller, reusable components. Each LWC is self-contained, encapsulating its functionality and styles.

Reusability and Modularity: LWC promotes reusability by providing a modular approach to component development. You can easily reuse LWCs across different projects and even share them with other developers.

Lightning Data Service Integration: LWC seamlessly integrates with Lightning Data Service, enabling efficient data retrieval and manipulation without writing Apex code. LWCs can interact with Salesforce records and utilize declarative features like record caching, error handling, and sharing rules.

Event-Driven Communication: LWCs communicate with each other using events. Events allow components to pass data and trigger actions between one another, facilitating interaction and coordination.

Section 2: Creating a Lightning Web Component

Let's create a simple Lightning Web Component to get started. Follow these steps:

Set Up the Development Environment: Ensure you have the necessary tools installed, such as Node.js and the Salesforce CLI.

Create a New LWC: Use the Salesforce CLI to create a new LWC project. Open your command-line interface and run the following commands:

```
sfdx force:project:create -n MyLWCProject

cd MyLWCProject

sfdx force:lightning:component:create -n HelloWorld -d force-app/main/default/lwc
```

Write the Component Code: Open the HelloWorld folder created in the previous step and modify the HelloWorld.js and HelloWorld.html files to define the behavior and markup of the component.

Add Styling (Optional): If desired, create a CSS file for styling the component. You can add it to the HelloWorld folder and reference it in the HelloWorld.js file.

Deploy the Component: Use the Salesforce CLI to deploy the component to your Salesforce org. Run the following command:

```
sfdx force:source:deploy -p force-
app/main/default/lwc/HelloWorld
```

Add the Component to a Visualforce Page: Create a Visualforce page and include the Lightning Web Component using the <c:HelloWorld> syntax.

Section 3: Interacting with Lightning Web Components

LWCs can communicate with each other and interact with the Salesforce platform. Here are some common interaction patterns:

Event Communication: Use events to communicate between LWCs. Define custom events in your LWCs and fire them using the dispatchEvent method. Other components can listen for these events and respond accordingly.

Apex Integration: LWCs can invoke Apex methods using the @AuraEnabled annotation. This enables LWCs to interact with the server-side logic and retrieve or modify data.

Lightning Data Service Integration: Utilize Lightning Data Service to work with Salesforce data. LWCs can use the force:recordData component or the lightning/uiRecordApi module to retrieve, create, update, or delete records.

Section 4: Best Practices for Lightning Web Components

Consider the following best practices when working with Lightning Web Components:

Follow the Single Responsibility Principle (SRP) by keeping your components focused on specific tasks or functionality.

Leverage reusability by designing components to be modular and independent, allowing for easy integration into different projects.

Utilize the Lightning Design System (SLDS) to maintain a consistent look and feel with Salesforce's UI.

Write clean and readable code by following JavaScript best practices, using proper naming conventions, and organizing your codebase effectively.

Thoroughly test your components using the Jest testing framework or other testing tools provided by the LWC framework.

Congratulations! You have learned the basics of Lightning Web Components (LWC) and how to create and interact with them. In the next chapter, we will delve deeper into LWC development techniques, exploring advanced features and customization options. Get ready to become a proficient LWC developer!

Chapter 15: Advanced Lightning Web Components (LWC) Development

Welcome to Chapter 15 of "Mastering Salesforce Visualforce: A Comprehensive Guide to Developing Custom User Interfaces." In this chapter, we will explore advanced Lightning Web Components (LWC) development techniques. We will delve deeper into LWC features and customization options to help you become a proficient LWC developer. Let's dive in!

Section 1: LWC Lifecycle Hooks

LWC provides a set of lifecycle hooks that allow you to perform actions at different stages of a component's lifecycle. Understanding these hooks is crucial for implementing complex functionality and ensuring efficient component behavior. Let's explore some essential lifecycle hooks:

constructor(): The constructor is called when the component is created but before it is inserted into the DOM. This is a good place to initialize variables and perform one-time setup tasks.

connectedCallback(): The connectedCallback is invoked when the component is inserted into the DOM. Use this hook to perform initialization tasks that require access to the component's rendered elements.

renderedCallback(): The renderedCallback is called whenever the component is rendered or re-rendered. Use this hook to perform tasks after the component has been rendered, such as manipulating the DOM or interacting with child components.

disconnectedCallback(): The disconnectedCallback is triggered when the component is removed from the DOM. Clean up any resources, event listeners, or subscriptions in this hook.

Section 2: LWC Communication Patterns

LWC provides multiple communication patterns to facilitate interaction between components. Understanding these patterns is essential for building complex applications with interconnected components. Let's explore some common communication patterns:

Parent-to-Child Communication: Pass data from a parent component to a child component using component attributes. Define attributes in the child component's JavaScript file and bind values to them in the parent component's HTML markup.

Child-to-Parent Communication: Emit custom events from a child component to notify its parent component about specific actions or changes. The parent component can listen for these events using the on directive and handle them accordingly.

Component Composition: Compose larger components by nesting child components within parent components. This allows you to break down complex functionality into smaller, reusable units.

Lightning Message Service: Utilize the Lightning Message Service to enable communication between unrelated components. Components can publish and subscribe to messages, allowing them to communicate without direct parent-child relationships.

Section 3: Styling and CSS Customization

LWC provides various options for styling and customizing the appearance of your components. Let's explore some techniques for styling LWC components:

Inline Styles: Apply inline styles directly to your component's HTML elements using the style attribute. This allows you to specify CSS properties and values inline.

CSS Classes: Define CSS classes in your component's CSS file and apply them to HTML elements using the class attribute. This promotes consistency and reusability across your components.

Scoped CSS: LWC provides native support for scoped CSS, ensuring that styles defined within a component only apply to its elements. Use the :host pseudo-class to style the component's root element.

External Stylesheets: Leverage external CSS files by importing them into your component's JavaScript file using the import statement. This allows you to organize and reuse CSS styles across multiple components.

Section 4: Testing Lightning Web Components

Testing is a crucial part of the development process, ensuring the functionality and stability of your Lightning Web Components. LWC provides robust testing capabilities to help you write effective unit tests. Let's explore some testing techniques:

Jest Testing Framework: LWC uses the Jest testing framework for unit testing. Jest provides a comprehensive set of testing utilities and features like test runners, assertions, and mocking capabilities.

Writing Unit Tests: Write unit tests for your components to verify their behavior and ensure they produce the expected output. Use Jest's describe and it functions to structure your tests and write assertions to validate component behavior.

Mocking Data and Dependencies: Use Jest's mocking capabilities to mock data and dependencies in your tests. This allows you to control the test environment and isolate component behavior.

Test Coverage and Code Quality: Aim for high test coverage to ensure that your components are thoroughly tested.

Monitor code quality using tools like code analyzers and linters to enforce best practices and maintain clean code.

Section 5: Performance Optimization

Optimizing the performance of your Lightning Web Components is crucial for delivering a smooth user experience. Consider the following techniques for performance optimization:

Debouncing and Throttling: Use techniques like debouncing and throttling to limit the frequency of event handlers and reduce unnecessary processing. This can prevent excessive updates and improve overall performance.

Conditional Rendering: Utilize conditional rendering to render components or parts of components only when necessary. This can reduce the initial rendering time and improve the perceived performance.

Data Caching and Lazy Loading: Implement caching mechanisms to avoid redundant data requests. Additionally, consider lazy loading techniques to load data or components on-demand as the user interacts with the interface.

Minification and Code Splitting: Minify your JavaScript and CSS files to reduce their file sizes. Consider code splitting techniques to load components or modules asynchronously, optimizing the initial load time.

Section 6: Best Practices for Lightning Web Components Development

Consider the following best practices to enhance your Lightning Web Components development:

Follow modular and reusable component design principles to promote code reusability and maintainability.

Separate business logic from presentation logic by encapsulating complex functionality within separate JavaScript modules.

Leverage standard Salesforce APIs and platform features, such as Lightning Data Service, for data manipulation and record access.

Write clear and concise documentation for your components, including usage instructions, input/output descriptions, and sample code snippets.

Stay updated with the latest LWC features, updates, and best practices by exploring the Salesforce documentation and developer resources.

Congratulations! You have learned advanced Lightning Web Components (LWC) development techniques. In the next chapter, we will explore the Lightning App Builder and how you can leverage it to create custom user interfaces without code. Get ready to build visually appealing applications with ease using the Lightning App Builder!

www.ingramcontent.com/pod-product-compliance
Lightning Source LLC
LaVergne TN
LVHW051717050326
832903LV00032B/4254